SELECTED POEMS

by Lawrence Durrell

SELECTED POEMS

OF

LAWRENCE DURRELL

Selected and with an Introduction by

ALAN ROSS

FABER AND FABER

3 Queen Square

London

First published in 1977
by Faber and Faber Limited
3 Queen Square London WC1
Printed in Great Britain by
Redwood Burn, Trowbridge
All rights reserved

British Library Cataloguing in Publication Data
Durrell, Lawrence
Selected poems of Lawrence Durrell
I. Ross, Alan
821'.9'12   PR6007.U76A17

ISBN 0 571 04943 5
ISBN 0 571 04944 3 Pbk

CONTENTS

INTRODUCTION

The poems in this volume have been arranged (with a number of exceptions noted in the list of contents) in chronological order of original volume publication. Of the order within the volumes themselves Lawrence Durrell has said '...I have always tried to arrange my poems for balanced readability – like one does a vase of flowers. How silly it would be to arrange the flowers in the order of their picking....' However, the chronology, in relation to Durrell's prose, is of some consequence. The first book from which they are taken, *A Private Country*, was published in 1943, the last, *Vega*, in 1973. Although Lawrence Durrell has written prose continuously since *The Black Book*, published in Paris in 1938, it was initially as a poet that he made an impact. *A Private Country* precedes the first of his island books *Prospero's Cell*, about Corfu, by two years. There followed two further volumes of poems, *Cities, Plains and People* and *On Seeming to Presume*, before the publication in 1953 of *Reflections on a Marine Venus*. Durrell's fourth book of poems *The Tree of Idleness* appeared in 1955, followed two years later by his Cyprus book *Bitter Lemons*. In that year, 1957, *Justine*, the first of the four novels comprising the *Alexandria Quartet*, was also published. *Clea*, the last of them, appeared in 1960, six years before the fifth volume of poems, *The Ikons*. By that time Durrell's reputation as a major novelist was established. His poems when they continued to appear seemed almost incidental to the preoccupations of his novels, to be more in the nature of notes in the margin. These Selected Poems will, I hope, adjust that impression.

The number of genuine poet-novelists, or novelist-poets for that matter, in this or any other century, can be counted on the fingers of one hand. It is inevitable that, from time to time, such a writer should appear to become involved with one kind of writing at the expense of the other. Since the Alexandrian novels of the late 1950s Durrell's earlier achievements as a poet have tended to be neglected. It is true, too, that in the succeeding years he has published considerably more prose than poetry. But anyone reading the fifty or so poems selected here from so many times that number will not need further reminder of his exceptional gifts. These are not only lyrical – no one has written more mnemonically about landscape, especially the Eastern Mediterranean – but classically allusive, epigrammatic and anecdotal. They range from affecting and beautiful love poems to skilful, succinct portraits and robust ballads. All his poems are firmly set in a historic perspective that enables him to move freely and comfortably in different countries at different times. His poetry is rich in ideas and subtle in his manipulation of them.

In comparison to the low-key and austere provincialism of much contemporary English verse, Durrell's natural exuberance and expatriate romantic melancholy may seem to some lushly cosmopolitan, but his most typical poems convey the excitement and sense of wonder that are the sources of myth and legend. At their simplest they quicken the heartbeat, restore the possibilities of human adventure.

In selecting these poems I have made no attempt to give equal emphasis to all aspects of Durrell's work. After many re-readings, I have made a purely personal choice from those that over thirty years seem to me to hold up best.

ALAN ROSS

A Private Country

[1943]

TO PING-KÛ, ASLEEP

You sleeping child asleep, away
Between the confusing world of forms,
The lamplight and the day; you lie
And the pause flows through you like glass,
Asleep in the body of the nautilus.

Between comparison and sleep,
Lips that move in quotation;
The turning of a small blind mind
Like a plant everywhere ascending.
Now our love has become a beanstalk.

Invent a language where the terms
Are smiles; someone in the house now
Only understands warmth and cherish,
Still twig-bound, learning to fly.

This hand exploring the world makes
The diver's deep-sea fingers on the sills
Of underwater windows; all the wrecks
Of our world where the sad blood leads back
Through memory and sense like divers working.

Sleep, my dear, we won't disturb
You, lying in the zones of sleep.
The four walls symbolise love put about
To hold in silence which so soon brims
Over into sadness: it's still dark.

Sleep and rise a lady with a flower
Between your teeth and a cypress
Between your thighs: surely you won't ever
Be puzzled by a poem or disturbed by a poem
Made like fire by the rubbing of two sticks?

'JE EST UN AUTRE'

—Rimbaud

He is the man who makes notes,
The observer in the tall black hat,
Face hidden in the brim:
In three European cities
He has watched me watching him.

The street-corner in Buda and after
By the post-office a glimpse
Of the disappearing tails of his coat,
Gave the same illumination, spied upon,
The tightness in the throat.

Once too meeting by the Seine
The waters a moving floor of stars,
He had vanished when I reached the door,
But there on the pavement burning
Lay one of his familiar black cigars.

The meeting on the dark stairway
Where the tide ran clean as a loom:
The betrayal of her, her kisses
He has witnessed them all: often
I hear him laughing in the other room.

He watches me now, working late,
Bringing a poem to life, his eyes
Reflect the malady of De Nerval:
O useless in this old house to question
The mirrors, his impenetrable disguise.

NEMEA

A song in the valley of Nemea:
Sing quiet, quite quiet here.

Song for the brides of Argos
Combing the swarms of golden hair:
Quite quiet, quiet there.

Under the rolling comb of grass,
The sword outrusts the golden helm.

Agamemnon under tumulus serene
Outsmiles the jury of skeletons:
Cool under cumulus the lion queen:

Only the drum can celebrate,
Only the adjective outlive them.

A song in the valley of Nemea:
Sing quiet, quiet, quiet here.

Tone of the frog in the empty well,
Drone of the bald bee on the cold skull,

Quiet, Quiet, Quiet.

A BALLAD OF THE GOOD LORD NELSON

The Good Lord Nelson had a swollen gland,
Little of the scripture did he understand
Till a woman led him to the promised land
    Aboard the Victory, Victory O.

Adam and Evil and a bushel of figs
Meant nothing to Nelson who was keeping pigs,
Till a woman showed him the various rigs
    Aboard the Victory, Victory O.

His heart was softer than a new laid egg,
Too poor for loving and ashamed to beg,
Till Nelson was taken by the Dancing Leg
    Aboard the Victory, Victory O.

Now he up and did up his little tin trunk
And he took to the ocean on his English junk,
Turning like the hour-glass in his lonely bunk
    Aboard the Victory, Victory O.

The Frenchman saw him a-coming there
With the one-piece eye and the valentine hair,
With the safety-pin sleeve and occupied air
    Aboard the Victory, Victory O.

Now you all remember the message he sent
As an answer to Hamilton's discontent—
There were questions asked about it in Parliament
    Aboard the Victory, Victory O.

Now the blacker the berry, the thicker comes the juice.
Think of Good Lord Nelson and avoid self-abuse,
For the empty sleeve was no mere excuse
    Aboard the Victory, Victory O.

'England Expects' was the motto he gave
When he thought of little Emma out on Biscay's wave,
And remembered working on her like a galley-slave
    Aboard the Victory, Victory O.

The first Great Lord in our English land
To honour the Freudian command,
For a cast in the bush is worth two in the hand
    Aboard the Victory, Victory O.

Now the Frenchman shot him there as he stood
In the rage of battle in a silk-lined hood
And he heard the whistle of his own hot blood
    Aboard the Victory, Victory O.

Now stiff on a pillar with a phallic air
Nelson stylites in Trafalgar Square
Reminds the British what once they were
    Aboard the Victory, Victory O.

If they'd treat their women in the Nelson way
There'd be fewer frigid husbands every day
And many more heroes on the Bay of Biscay
    Aboard the Victory, Victory O.

Cities, Plains and People

[1946]

WATER MUSIC

Wrap your sulky beauty up,
From sea-fever, from winterfall
Out of the swing of the
Swing of the sea.

Keep safe from noonfall,
Starlight and smokefall where
Waves roll, waves toll but feel
None of our roving fever.

From dayfever and nightsadness
Keep, bless, hold: from cold
Wrap your sulky beauty into sleep
Out of the swing of the
Swing of sea.

ON FIRST LOOKING INTO
LOEB'S HORACE

I found your Horace with the writing in it;
Out of time and context came upon
This lover of vines and slave to quietness,
Walking like a figure of smoke here, musing
Among his high and lovely Tuscan pines.

All the small-holder's ambitions; the yield
Of wine-bearing grape, pruning and drainage
Laid out by laws, almost like the austere
Shell of his verses—a pattern of Latin thrift;
Waiting so patiently in a library for
Autumn and the drying of the apples;
The betraying hour-glass and its deathward drift.

Surely the hard blue winterset
Must have conveyed a message to him—
The premonitions that the garden heard
Shrunk in its shirt of hair beneath the stars,
How rude and feeble a tenant was the self,
An Empire, the body with its members dying—
And unwhistling now the vanished Roman bird?

The fruit-trees dropping apples; he counted them;
The soft bounding fruit on leafy terraces,
And turned to the consoling winter rooms
Where, facing south, began the great prayer,
With his reed laid upon the margins
Of the dead, his stainless authors,
Upright, severe on an uncomfortable chair.

Here, where your clear hand marked up
'The hated cypress' I added 'Because it grew
On tombs, revealed his fear of autumn and the urns',
Depicting a solitary at an upper window
Revising metaphors for the winter sea: 'O
Dark head of storm-tossed curls'; or silently
Watching the North Star which like a fever burns

Away the envy and neglect of the common,
Shining on this terrace, lifting up in recreation
The sad heart of Horace who must have seen it only
As a metaphor for the self and its perfection—
A burning heart quite constant in its station.

Easy to be patient in the summer,
The light running like fishes among the leaves,
Easy in August with its cones of blue
Sky uninvaded from the north; but winter
With its bareness pared his words to points
Like stars, leaving them pure but very few.

He will not know how we discerned him, disregarding
The pose of sufficiency, the landed man,
Found a suffering limb on the great Latin tree
Whose roots live in the barbarian grammar we
Use, yet based in him, his mason's tongue;
Describing clearly a bachelor, sedentary,
With a fond weakness for bronze-age conversation,
Disguising a sense of failure in a hatred for the young,

Who built in the Sabine hills this forgery
Of completeness, an orchard with a view of Rome;
Who studiously developed his sense of death

Till it was all around him, walking at the circus,
At the baths, playing dominoes in a shop—
The escape from self-knowledge with its tragic
Imperatives: *Seek, suffer, endure*. The Roman
In him feared the Law and told him where to stop.

So perfect a disguise for one who had
Exhausted death in art—yet who could guess
You would discern the liar by a line,
The suffering hidden under gentleness
And add upon the flyleaf in your tall
Clear hand: 'Fat, human and unloved,
And held from loving by a sort of wall,
Laid down his books and lovers one by one,
Indifference and success had crowned them all.'

BYRON

The trees have been rapping
At these empty casements for a year,
Have been rapping and tapping and
Repeating to us here
Omens of the defeating wind,
Omens of the defeating mind.

Headquarters of a war
House in a fever-swamp
Headquarters of a mind at odds.

Before me now lies Byron and behind,
Belonging to the Gods,
Another Byron of the feeling
Shown in this barbered hairless man,
Splashed by the candle-stems
In his expensive cloak and wig
And boots upon the dirty ceiling.

Hobbled by this shadow,
My own invention of myself, I go
In wind, rain, stars, climbing
This ladder of compromises into Greece
Which like the Notself looms before
My politics, my invention and my war.
None of it but belongs
To this farded character
Whose Grecian credits are his old excuse
By freedom holding Byron in abuse.

Strange for one who was happier
Tuned to women, to seek and sift
In the heart's simple mesh,
To know so certainly
Under the perfume and the politics
What undertow of odours haunts the flesh:
Could once resume them all
In lines that gave me rest,
And watch the fat fly Death
Hunting the skeleton down in each,
Like hairs in plaster growing,
Promising under the living red the yellow—
I helped these pretty children by their sex
Discountenance the horrid fellow.

I have been a secretary (I sing)
A secretary to love . . .

In this bad opera landscape
Trees, fevers and quarrels
Spread like sores: while the gilded
Abstractions like our pride and honour
On this brute age close like doors
Which pushing does not budge.

Outside them, I speak for the great average.
My disobedience became
A disguise for a style in a new dress.
Item: a lock of hair.
Item: a miniature, myself aged three,
The innocent and the deformed
Pinned up in ribbons for posterity.

And now here comes
The famous disposition to weep,
To renounce. Picture to yourself
A lord who encircled his life
With women's arms; or another
Who rode through the wide world howling
And searching for his mother.

Picture to yourself a third: a cynic.
This weeping published rock—
The biscuits and the glass of soda-water:
Under Sunium's white cliffs
Where I laboured with my knife
To cut a 'Byron' there—
I was thinking softly of my daughter.

A cock to Aesculapius no less . . .

You will suggest we found only
In idleness and indignation here,
Plucked by the offshore dancers, brigs
Like girls, and ports of call
In our commerce with liberty, the Whore,
Through these unbarbered priests
And garlic-eating captains:
Fame like the only porch in a wall
To squeeze our shelter from
By profit and by circumstance
Assist this rocky nation's funeral.

The humane and the lawful in whom
Art and manners mix, who sent us here,
This sort of figures from a drawing-room

Should be paused themselves once
Under these legendary islands.
A landscape hurled into the air
And fallen on itself: we should see
Where the frail spines of rivers
Soft on the backbone intersect and scribble
These unbarbered gangs of freedom dribble
Like music down a page and come
Into the valleys with their small
Ordnance which barks and jumps.
I, Byron: the soft head of my heart bumps
Inside me as on a vellum drum.

Other enemies intervene here,
Not less where the valet serves
In a muddle of papers and consequences;
Not less in places where I walk alone
With Conscience, the defective: my defences
Against a past which lies behind,
Writing and rewriting to the bone
Those famous letters in my mind.

Time grows short. Now the trees
Are rapping at the empty casements.
Fevers are closing in on us at last—
So long desired an end of service
To the flesh and its competitions of endurance.
There is so little time. Fletcher
Tidies the bed at dusk and brings me coffee.

You, the speaking and the feeling who come after:
I sent you something once—it must be
Somewhere in *Juan*—it has not reached you yet.

O watch for this remote
But very self of Byron and of me,
Blown empty on the white cliffs of the mind,
A dispossessed His Lordship writing you
A message in a bottle dropped at sea.

ALEXANDRIA

To the lucky now who have lovers or friends,
Who move to their sweet undiscovered ends,
Or whom the great conspiracy deceives,
I wish these whirling autumn leaves:
Promontories splashed by the salty sea,
Groaned on in darkness by the tram
To horizons of love or good luck or more love—
As for me I now move
Through many negatives to what I am.

Here at the last cold Pharos between Greece
And all I love, the lights confide
A deeper darkness to the rubbing tide;
Doors shut, and we the living are locked inside
Between the shadows and the thoughts of peace:
And so in furnished rooms revise
The index of our lovers and our friends
From gestures possibly forgotten, but the ends
Of longings like unconnected nerves,
And in this quiet rehearsal of their acts
We dream of them and cherish them as Facts.

Now when the sea grows restless as a conscript,
Excited by fresh wind, climbs the sea-wall,
I walk by it and think about you all:
B. with his respect for the Object, and D.
Searching in sex like a great pantry for jars
Marked 'Plum and apple'; and the small, fell
Figure of Dorian ringing like a muffin-bell—
All indeed whom war or time threw up
On this littoral and tides could not move
Were objects for my study and my love.

And then turning where the last pale
Lighthouse, like a Samson blinded, stands
And turns its huge charred orbit on the sands
I think of you—indeed mostly of you,
In whom a writer would only name and lose
The dented boy's lip and the close
Archer's shoulders; but here to rediscover
By tides and faults of weather, by the rain
Which washes everything, the critic and the lover.

At the doors of Africa so many towns founded
Upon a parting could become Alexandria, like
The wife of Lot—a metaphor for tears;
And the queer student in his poky hot
Tenth floor room above the harbour hears
The sirens shaking the tree of his heart,
And shuts his books, while the most
Inexpressible longings like wounds unstitched
Stir in him some girl's unquiet ghost.

So we, learning to suffer and not condemn
Can only wish you this great pure wind
Condemned by Greece, and turning like a helm
Inland where it smokes the fires of men,
Spins weathercocks on farms or catches
The lovers at their quarrel in the sheets;
Or like a walker in the darkness might,
Knocks and disturbs the artist at his papers
Up there alone, upon the alps of night.

DELOS

For Diana Gould

On charts they fall like lace,
Islands consuming in a sea
Born dense with its own blue:
And like repairing mirrors holding up
Small towns and trees and rivers
To the still air, the lovely air:
From the clear side of springing Time,
In clement places where the windmills ride,
Turning over grey springs in Mykonos,
In shadows with a gesture of content.

The statues of the dead here
Embark on sunlight, sealed
Each in her model with the sightless eyes:
The modest stones of Greeks,
Who gravely interrupted death by pleasure.

And in harbours softly fallen
The liver-coloured sails—
Sharp-featured brigantines with eyes—
Ride in reception so like women:
The pathetic faculty of girls
To register and utter a desire
In the arms of men upon the new-mown waters,
Follow the wind, with their long shining keels
Aimed across Delos at a star.

POGGIO

The rubber penis, the wig, the false breasts . . .
The talent for entering rooms backwards
Upon a roar of laughter, with his dumb
Pained expression, wheeling there before him
That mythological great hippo's bum:

'Who should it be but Poggio?' The white face,
Comical, flat, and hairless as a cheese.
Nose like a member: something worn:
A Tuscan fig, a leather can, or else,
A phallus made of putty and slapped on.

How should you know that behind
All this the old buffoon concealed a fear—
And reasonable enough—that he might be
An artist after all? Always after this kind
Of side-splitting evening, sitting there
On a three-legged stool and writing, he

Hoped poems might form upon the paper.
But no. Dirty stories. The actress and the bishop.
The ape and the eunuch. This crapula clung
To him for many years between his dinners . . .
He sweated at them like a ham unhung.

And like the rest of us hoped for
The transfigured story or the mantic line
Of poetry free from this mortuary smell.
For years slept badly—who does not?
Took bribes, and drugs, ate far too much and dreamed.
Married unwisely, yes, but died quite well.

MYTHOLOGY

Miss Willow, secretly known as 'tit' . . .
Plotkin who slipped on new ice
And wounded the stinks master
The winter when the ponds froze over . . .

Square roots of the symbol Abraham
Cut off below the burning bush,
Or in the botany classes heads
Drying between covers like rare ferns,
Stamen and pistil, we were young then.

Later with tunes like 'Hips and Whores'
The song-book summed us up,
Mixing reality with circumstance,
With Hotchkiss cock of the walk
Top button undone, and braided cap,
He was the way and the life.

What dismays is not time
Assuaging every thirst with a surprise,
Bitterness hidden in desiring bodies,
Unfolded strictly, governed by the germ.

Plotkin cooked like a pie in iron lungs:
Glass rods the doctors dipped in burning nitrates
Dripped scalding on in private hospitals
And poor 'tit' Willow who had been
Young, pretty and perhaps contemptuous
Dreaming of love, was carried to Spain in a cage.

On Seeming to Presume

[1948]

GREEN COCONUTS: RIO

At insular café tables under awnings
Bemused benighted half-castes pause
To stretch upon a table yawning
Ten yellow claws and
Order green coconuts to drink with straws.

Milk of the green loaf-coconuts
Which soon before them amputated stand,
Broken, you think, from some great tree of breasts,
Or the green skulls of savages trepanned.

Lips that are curved to taste this albumen,
To dredge with some blue spoon among the curds
Which drying on tongue or on moustache are tasteless
As droppings of bats or birds.

Re-enacting here a theory out of Darwin
They cup their yellow mandibles to shape
Their nuts, tilt them in drinking poses,
To drain them slowly from the very nape:
Green coconuts, green
Coconuts, patrimony of the ape.

BERE REGIS

The colonial, the expatriate walking here
Awkwardly enclosing the commonwealth of his love
Stoops to this lovely expurgated prose-land
Where winter with its holly locks the schools
And spring with nature improvises
With the thrush on ploughland, with the scarecrow.

Moss walls, woollen forests, Shakespear, desuetude:
Roots of his language as familiar as salt
Inhaling cattle lick in this mnemonic valley
Where the gnats assort, the thrush familiarises,
And over his cottage a colloquial moon.

SWANS

Fraudulent perhaps in that they gave
No sense of muscle but a swollen languor
Though moved by webs: yet idly, idly
As soap-bubbles drift from a clay-pipe
They mowed the lake in tapestry,

Passing in regal exhaustion by us,
King, queen and cygnets, one by one.
Did one dare to remember other swans
In anecdotes of Gauguin or of Rabelais?
Some became bolsters for the Greeks,
Some rubber Lohengrins provided comedy.
The flapping of the wings excited Leda.
The procession is over and what is now
Alarming is more the mirror split
From end to end by the harsh clap
Of the wooden beaks, than the empty space
Which follows them about,
Stained by their whiteness when they pass.

We sit like drunkards and inhale the swans.

BLIND HOMER

A winter night again, and the moon
Loosely inks in the marbles and retires.

The six pines whistle and stretch and there,
Eastward the loaded brush of morning pauses

Where the few Grecian stars sink and revive
Each night in glittering baths of sound.

Now to the winter each has given up
Deciduous stuff, the snakeskin and the antler,

Cast skin of poetry and the grape.

Blind Homer, the lizards still sup the heat
From the rocks, and still the spring,

Noiseless as coins on hair repeats
Her diphthong after diphthong endlessly.

Exchange a glance with one whose art
Conspires with introspection against loneliness

This February 1946, pulse normal, nerves at rest:
Heir to a like disorder, only lately grown

Much more uncertain of his gift with words,
By this plate of olives, this dry inkwell.

RODINI

Windless plane-trees above Rodini
To the pencil or the eye are tempters

Where of late trees have become ears in leaf
Curved for the cicada's first monotony.

Hollow the comb, mellow the sweetness
Amber the honey-spoil, drink, drink.

In these windless unechoing valleys
The mind slips like a chisel-hand

Touching the surface of this clement blue
Yet must not damage the solitary Turk

Gathering his team and singing, in whose brain
The same disorder and the loneliness—

The what-we-have-in-common of us all.
Is there enough perhaps to found a world?

Then of what you said once, the passing
Of something on the road beyond the tombstones

Reflecting on dark hair with its sudden theft
Of blue from the darkness of violets

And below the nape of the neck a mole
All mixed in this odourless water-clock of hours.

43

So one is grateful, yes, to the ancient Greeks
For the invention of time, lustration of penitents,

Not so much for what they were
But for where we lie under the windless planes.

THE DAILY MIRROR

Writing this stuff should not have been like
Suicide over some ordinary misapprehension:

A man going into his own house, say,
Turning out all the lights before undressing,

At the bedside of some lovely ignoramus
Whispering: 'Tomorrow I swear is the last time.'

Or: 'Believe, and I swear you will never die.'
This nib dragged out like the late train

Racing on iron bars for the north.
Target: another world, not necessarily better,

Of course, but different, completely different.
The hour-glass shifting its trash of seconds.

If it does not end this way perhaps some other.
Gossip lying in a furnished room, blinds drawn.

A poem with its throat cut from ear to ear.

The Tree of Idleness

[1955]

LESBOS

The Pleiades are sinking calm as paint,
And earth's huge camber follows out,
Turning in sleep, the oceanic curve,

Defined in concave like a human eye
Or cheek pressed warm on the dark's cheek,
Like dancers to a music they deserve.

This balcony, a moon-anointed shelf
Above a silent garden holds my bed.
I slept. But the dispiriting autumn moon,

In her slow expurgation of the sky
Needs company: is brooding on the dead,
And so am I now, so am I.

CHANEL

Scent like a river-pilot led me there:
Bedroom darkness spreading like a moss,
The polished wells of floors in blackness
Gave no reflections of the personage,
Or the half-open door, but whispered on:

'Skin be supple, hair be smooth,
Lips and character attend
In mnemonic solitude.
Kisses leave no fingerprints.'
'Answer.' But no answer came.
'Beauty hunted leaves no clues.'

Yet as if rising from a still,
Perfume whispered at the sill,
All those discarded husks of thought
Hanging untenanted like gowns,
Rinds of which the fruit had gone . . .

Still the long chapter led me on.
Still the clock beside the bed
Heart-beat after heart-beat shed.

A PORTRAIT OF THEODORA

I recall her by a freckle of gold
In the pupil of one eye, an odd
Strawberry-gold: and after many years
Of forgetting that musical body—
Arms too long, wrists too slender—
Remember only the unstable wishes
Disquieting the flesh. I will not
Deny her pomp was laughable, urban:
Behind it one could hear the sad
Provincial laughter rotted by insomnia.

None of these meetings are planned,
I guess, or willed by the exemplars
Of a city's love—a city founded in
The name of love: to me is always
Brown face, white teeth, cheap summer frock
In green and white stripes and then
Forever a strawberry eye. I recalled no more
For years. The eye was lying in wait.

Then in another city from the same
Twice-used air and sheets, in the midst
Of a parting: the same dark bedroom,
Arctic chamber-pot and cruel iron bed,
I saw the street-lamp unpick Theodora
Like an old sweater, unwrinkle eyes and mouth,
Unbandaging her youth to let me see
The wounds I had not understood before.

How could I have ignored such wounds?
The bloody sweepings of a loving smile
Strewed like Osiris among the dunes?
Now only my experience recognizes her
Too late, among the other great survivors
Of the city's rage, and places her among
The champions of love—among the true elect!

SARAJEVO

Bosnia. November. And the mountain roads
Earthbound but matching perfectly these long
And passionate self-communings counter-march,
Balanced on scarps of trap, ramble or blunder
Over traverses of cloud: and here they move,
Mule-teams like insects harnessed by a bell
Upon the leaf-edge of a winter sky,

And down at last into this lap of stone
Between four cataracts of rock: a town
Peopled by sleepy eagles, whispering only
Of the sunburnt herdsman's hopeless ploy:
A sterile earth quickened by shards of rock
Where nothing grows, not even in his sleep,

Where minarets have twisted up like sugar
And a river, curdled with blond ice, drives on
Tinkling among the mule-teams and the mountaineers,
Under the bridges and the wooden trellises
Which tame the air and promise us a peace
Harmless with nightingales. None are singing now.

No history much? Perhaps. Only this ominous
Dark beauty flowering under veils,
Trapped in the spectrum of a dying style:
A village like an instinct left to rust,
Composed around the echo of a pistol-shot.

STYLE

Something like the sea,
Unlaboured momentum of water
But going somewhere,
Building and subsiding,
The busy one, the loveless.

Or the wind that slits
Forests from end to end,
Inspiriting vast audiences,
Ovations of leafy hands
Accepting, accepting.

But neither is yet
Fine enough for the line I hunt.
The dry bony blade of the
Sword-grass might suit me
Better: an assassin of polish.

Such a bite of perfect temper
As unwary fingers provoke,
Not to be felt till later,
Turning away, to notice the thread
Of blood from its unfelt stroke.

THE DYING FALL

The islands rebuffed by water.
Estuaries of putty and gold.
A smokeless arc of Latin sky.
One star, less than a week old.

Memory now, I lead her haltered.
Stab of the opiate in the arm
When the sea wears bronze scales and
Hushes in the ambush of a calm.

The old dialogue always rebegins
Between us: but now the spring
Ripens, neither will be attending,
For rosy as feet of pigeons pressed

In clay, the kisses we possessed,
Or thought we did: so borrowing, lending,
Stacked fortunes in our love's society—
Each in the perfect circle of a sigh was ending.

THE TREE OF IDLENESS

I shall die one day I suppose
In this old Turkish house I inhabit:
A ragged banana-leaf outside and here
On the sill in a jam-jar a rock-rose.

Perhaps a single pining mandolin
Throbs where cicadas have quarried
To the heart of all misgiving and there
Scratches on silence like a pet locked in.

Will I be more or less dead
Than the village in memory's dispersing
Springs, or in some cloud of witness see,
Looking back, the selfsame road ahead?

By the moist clay of a woman's wanting,
After the heart has stopped its fearful
Gnawing, will I descry between
This life and that another sort of haunting?

No: the card-players in tabs of shade
Will play on: the aerial springs
Hiss: in bed lying quiet under kisses
Without signature, with all my debts unpaid

I shall recall nights of squinting rain,
Like pig-iron on the hills: bruised
Landscapes of drumming cloud and everywhere
The lack of someone spreading like a stain.

Or where brown fingers in the darkness move,
Before the early shepherds have awoken,
Tap out on sleeping lips with these same
Worn typewriter keys a poem imploring

Silence of lips and minds which have not spoken.

A WATER-COLOUR OF VENICE

Zarian was saying: Florence is youth,
And after it Ravenna, age,
Then Venice, second-childhood.

The pools of burning stone where time
And water, the old siege-masters,
Have run their saps beneath
A thousand saddle-bridges,
Puffed up by marble griffins drinking,

And all set free to float on loops
Of her canals like great intestines
Now snapped off like a berg to float,
Where now, like others, you have come alone,
To trap your sunset in a yellow glass,
And watch the silversmith at work
Chasing the famous salver of the bay . . .

Here sense dissolves, combines to print only
These bitten choirs of stone on water,
To the rumble of old cloth bells,
The cadging of confetti pigeons,
A boatman singing from his long black coffin . . .

To all that has been said before
You can add nothing, only that here,
Thick as a brushstroke sleep has laid
Its fleecy unconcern on every visage,

At the bottom of every soul a spoonful of sleep.

The Ikons

[1966]

STONE HONEY

Reading him is to refresh all nature,
Where, newly elaborated, reality attends.
The primal innocence in things confronting
His eye as thoughtful, innocence as unstudied . . .
One could almost say holy in the scientific sense.
So while renewing nature he relives for us
The simple things our inattention staled,
Noting sagely how water can curl like hair,
Its undisciplined recoil moving mountains
Or drumming out geysers in the earth's crust,
Or the reflex stroke which buries ancient cities.

But water was only one of the things Leonardo
Was keen on, liked to sit down and draw.
It would not stay still; and sitting there beside
The plate of olives, the comb of stone honey,
Which seemed so eternal in the scale of values,
So philosophically immortal, he was touched
By the sense of time's fragility, the semen of fate.
The adventitious seconds, days or seasons,
Though time stood still some drowsy afternoon,
Became for him dense, gravid with their futurity.
Life was pitiless after all, advancing and recoiling
Like the seas of the mind. The only purchase was
This, deliberately to make the time to note:
'The earth is budged from its position by the
Merest weight of a little bird alighting on it.'

IO

In the museums you can find her,
Io, the contemporary street-walker all alive
In bronze and leather, spear in hand,
Her hair packed in some slender helm
Like a tall golden hive—
A fresco of a parody of arms.
Or else on vases rushing to overwhelm
Invaders of the olive or the attic farms:
Reviving warriors, helmets full of water,
Or kneeling to swarthy foreigners,
A hostage, someone's youngest daughter.
All the repulsion and the joy in one.

Well, all afternoon I've reflected on Athens,
The slim statue asleep over there,
Without unduly stressing the classical pallor
Or the emphatic disabused air
Street-girls have asleep; no,
All that will keep, all that will keep.
Soon we must be exiled to different corners
Of the sky; but the inward whiteness harms not
With dark keeping, harms not. Yet perhaps
I should sneak out and leave her here asleep?
Draw tight those arms like silver toils
The Parcae weave as their supreme award
And between deep drawn breaths release
The flying bolt of the unuttered word.

VIDOURLE

River the Roman legionary noosed:
Seven piers whose sharpened fangs
Slide from stone gums to soothe and comb
Where the lustrous nervous water hangs.
A stagnant town: a someone's home-from-home.
If the bored consular ghost should reappear
He would re-pose the question with a sigh,
Find it unanswered still: 'What under heaven
Could a Roman find to amuse him here?'
It won't: he's gone on furlough unregretted,
Now powdered with drowsy lilies, hobbled,
Dusted by old Orion the glib waterfloor
A planet-cobbled darkness re-inters
The history the consul found a bore.

Pour sky in water, softly mix and wait,
While birds whistle and sprain and curve . . .
They must have faltered here at the very gate
Of Gaul, seduced by such provender, such rich turf
Bewitched, and made their sense of duty swerve.
No less now under awnings half asleep
Pale functionaries of a similar sort of creed
All afternoon a river-watching keep,
Two civil servants loitering over aniseed.

A PERSIAN LADY

Some diplomatic mission—no such thing as 'fate'—
Brought her to the city that ripening spring.
She was much pointed out—a Lady-in-Waiting—
To some Persian noble; well, and here she was
Merry and indolent amidst fashionable abundance.
By day under a saffron parasol on royal beaches,
By night in a queer crocked tent with tassels.

He noted the perfected darkness of her beauty,
The mind recoiling as from a branding-iron:
The sea advancing and retiring at her lacquered toes;
How would one say 'to enflame' in her tongue,
He wondered, knowing it applied to female beauty?
When their eyes met he felt dis-figured
It would have been simple—three paces apart!

Disloyal time! They let the seminal instant go,
The code unbroken, the collision of ripening wishes
Abandoned to hiss on in the great syllabaries of memory.
Next day he deliberately left the musical city
To join a boring water-party on the lake.
Telling himself 'Say what you like about it,
I have been spared very much in this business.'

He meant, I think, that never should he now
Know the slow disgracing of her mind, the slow
Spiral of her beauty's deterioration, flagging desires,
The stagnant fury of the temporal yoke,
Grey temple, long slide into fat.

On the other hand neither would she build him sons
Or be a subject for verses—the famished in-bred poetry
Which was the fashion of his time and ours.
She would exist, pure, symmetrical and intact
Like the sterile hyphen which divides and joins
In a biography the year of birth and death.

Vega
[1973]

THE RECKONING

Later some of these heroic worshippers
May live out one thrift in a world of options,
The crown of thorns, the bridal wreath of love,
Desires in all their motions.
'As below, darling, so above.'
In one thought focus and resume
The thousand contradictions,
And still with a sigh these warring fictions.

Timeless as water into language flowing,
Molten as snow on new burns,
The limbo of half-knowing
Where the gagged conscience twists and turns,
Will plant the flag of their unknowing.

It is not peace we seek but meaning.

To convince at last that all is possible,
That the feeble human finite must belong
Within the starry circumference of wonder,
And waking alone at night so suddenly
Realise how careful one must be with hate—
For you become what you hate too much,
As when you love too much you fraction
By insolence the fine delight . . .

It is not meaning that we need but sight.

NOBODY

You and who else?
Who else? Why Nobody.
I shall be weeks or months away now
Where the diving roads divide,
A solitude with little dignity,
Where forests lie, where rivers pine,
In a great hemisphere of loveless sky:
And your letters will cross mine.

Somewhere perhaps in a cobweb of skyscrapers
Between fifth and sixth musing I'll go,
Matching some footprints in young snow,
Within the loving ambush of some heart,
So close and yet so very far apart . . .
I don't know, I just don't know.

Two beings watching the spyscrapers fade,
Rose in the falling sleet or
Phantom green, licking themselves
Like great cats at their toilet,
Licking their paws clean.
I shall hesitate and falter, that much I know.

Moreover, do you suppose, you too
When you reach India at last, as you will,
I'll be back before two empty coffee cups
And your empty chair in our shabby bistro;
You'll have nothing to tell me either, no,
Not the tenth part of a sigh to exchange.
Everything will be just so.
I'll be back along again
Confined in memory, but nothing to report,
Watching the traffic pass and
Dreaming of footprints in the New York snow.

RAIN, RAIN, GO TO SPAIN

That noise will be the rain again,
Hush-falling absolver of together—
Companionable enough, though, here abroad:
The log fire, some conclusive music, loneliness.
I can visualise somebody at the door
But make no name or shape for such an image,
Just a locus for small thefts
As might love us both awake tomorrow,
An echo off the lead and ownerless.
But this hissing rain won't improve anything.
The roads will be washed out. Thinking falters.

My book-lined walls so scholarly,
So rosy, glassed in by the rain.
I finger the sex of many an uncut book.
Now spring is coming you will get home
Later and later in another climate.
You vanished so abruptly it took me by surprise.
I heard to relearn everything again
As if blinded by a life of tiny braille.

Then a whole year with just one card,
From Madrid. 'It is raining here and
Greco is so sombre. I have decided
At last to love nobody but myself.'
I repeat it in an amused way
Sometimes very late at night.
In an amazed way as anyone might
Looking up from a classic into all the
Marvellous rain-polished darkness.

As if suddenly you had gone
Beyond the twelfth desire:
You and memory both become
Contemporary to all this inner music.
Time to sift out our silences, then:
Time to relay the failing fire.

PISTOL WEATHER

About loving, and such kindred matters
You could be beguiling enough;
Delicacy, constancy and depth—
We examined every artificial prison,
And all with the necessary sincerity, yes.

Some languages have little euphemisms
Which modify suddenly one's notions,
Alter one's whole way of adoring:
Such as your character for 'death',
Which reads simply 'A stepping forever
Into a whiteness without remission.'
With no separation-anxiety I presume?

Surely to love is to coincide a little?
And after I contracted your own mightier
Loneliness, I became really ill myself.
But grateful for the thorny knowledge of you;
And thank you for the choice of time and place.

I would perhaps have asked you away
To my house by the sea, to revive us both,
In absolute solitude and dispassionately,
But all the time I kept seeing the severed head,
Lying there, eyes open, in your lap.

REVENANTS

Supposing once the dead were to combine
Against us with a disciplined hysteria.
Particular ghosts might then trouble
With professional horrors like
Corpses in evening dress,
Photoglyphs from some ancient calendar
Pictographs of lost time.
The smile frail as a toy night-light
Beside a sleeping infant's bed.
The pallor would be unfeigned,
The child smile in its sleep.

To see them always in memory
Descending a spiral staircase slowly
With that peculiar fond regard

Or else out in silent gardens
Under stone walls, a snapped fountain,
Wild violets there uncaring
Wild cyclamen uncurling
In silence, in loaf-leisure.

Or a last specialised picture
Flickering on the retina perhaps
The suave magnificence of a late
Moon, trying not to insist too much.
Emotions are just pampered mirrors,
Thriftless provinces, penurious settlers.
How to involve all nature in every breath?

AVIGNON

Come, meet me in some dead café—
A puff of cognac or a sip of smoke
Will grant a more prolific light,
Say there is nothing to revoke.

A veteran with no arm will press
A phantom sorrow in his sleeve;
The aching stump may well insist
On memories it can't relieve.

Late cats, the city's thumbscrews twist.
Night falls in its profuse derision,
Brings candle-power to younger lives,
Cancels in me the primal vision.

Come, random with me in the rain,
In ghastly harness like a dream,
In rainwashed streets of saddened dark
Where nothing moves that does not seem.

SWIMMERS

Huit heures . . . honte heures . . . supper will be cold.
Sex no substitute for
Science no worship for . . .
At night seeing lights and crouching
Figures round the swimming pool, rapt.
They were fishing for her pearls,
Her necklace had broken while she swam.
'Darling, I bust my pearls.'

But all the time I was away
In sweet and headlong Greece I tried
To write you only the syntax failed,
Each noun became a nascent verb
And all verbs dormant adjectives,
Everything sleeping among the scattered pearls.

Corpses with the marvellous
Property of withoutness
Reign in the whole abundance of the breath.
Each mood has its breathing, so does death.
Soft they sleep and corpsely wise
Scattered the pearls that were their eyes.
Newly mated man and wine
In each other's deaths combine.
Somebody meets everything
While poems in their cages sing.

MISTRAL

At four the dawn mistral usually
A sleep-walking giant sways and crackles
The house, a vessel big with sail.
One head full of poems, cruiser of light,
Cracks open the pomegranate to reveal
The lining of all today's perhapses.

Far away in her carnal fealty sleeps
La Môme in her tiny *chambre de bonne*.
'*Le vent se lève . . . Il faut tenter de vivre.*'

I have grave thoughts about nothingness,
Hold no copyright in Jesus like that girl.
An autopsy would fuse the wires of pleading.
It is simply not possible to thank life.
The universe seems a huge hug without arms.
In foul rapture dawn breaks on grey olives.
Poetry among other afflictions
Is the purest selfishness.

I am making her a small scarlet jazz
For the cellar where they dance
To a wheezy accordion, with a one-eyed man.
Written to a cheeky begging voice.

> *Moi je suis*
> *Annie Verneuil*
> *Dit Annie La Môme*
> *Parfois je fais la vie*
> *Parfois je chome*
> *Premier Prix de Saloperie*
> *De Paris à Rome*
> *Annie La Môme*
> *Fléau du flic le soir*

Sur La Place Vendôme,
Annie Verneuil
Annie La Môme

Freedom is choice: choice bondage.
Where will I next be when the mistral
Rises in sullen trumpets on the hills of bone?

ALPHABETA

Some withering papers lie,
The bloody spoor of some great
Animal anxiety of a poem he wounded
And followed up in fear, holding his breath.
The blood was everywhere, the yellowing inks
Of old manuscripts reproached.
In stark terror that loaded pen was ready,
With the safety catch turned off,
Only the target lacked,
Crouching somewhere in its own blood.
Some hideous animal without a name.
To be called man, but with such a rotten aim!

CONFEDERATE

At long last the wind has decided for itself,
Skies arch and glass panes shudder inwards,
My shutter croaks and now you tell me
It is time for those last few words. Very well.
Epoch of a whitewashed moon with
Frost in the bulb and the quailing local blood.
Very well; for not in this season will kisses
Dig any deeper into the mind to seek
The mislaid words we have been seeking,
Delegates of that place which once
The whole of suffering seemed to occupy—
O nothing really infernal, a simple darkness.
But because I came both grew abruptly .
Aware of all the surrounding armies
So many faces torn from the same world,
Whole lives lost by mere inattention.

SEFERIS

Time quietly compiling us like sheaves
Turns round one day, beckons the special few,
With one bird singing somewhere in the leaves,
Someone like K. or somebody like you,
Free-falling target for the envious thrust,
So tilting into darkness go we must.

Thus the fading writer signing off
Sees in the vast perspectives of dispersal
His words float off like tiny seeds,
Wind-borne or bird-distributed notes,
To the very end of loves without rehearsal,
The stinging image riper than his deeds.

Yours must have set out like ancient
Colonists, from Delos or from Rhodes,
To dare the sun-gods, found great entrepôts,
Naples or Rio, far from man's known abodes,
To confer the quaint Grecian script on other men;
A new Greek fire ignited by your pen.

How marvellous to have done it and then left
It in the lost property office of the loving mind,
The secret whisper those who listen find.
You show us all the way the great ones went,
In silences becalmed, so well they knew
That even to die is somehow to invent.

*Chronology and Volume Publication
Unknown*

MANOLI OF COS

Down there below the temple
Where the penitents scattered
Ashes of dead birds, Manoli goes
In his leaky boat, a rose tied to the rudder.

This is not the rose of all the world,
Nor the rose of Nostradamus or of Malory:
Nor is it Eliot's clear northern rose of the mind,
But precisely and unequivocally
The red rose Manoli picked himself
From the vocabulary of roses on the hill by Cefalù.

A RHODIAN CAPTAIN

Ten speechless knuckles lie along a knee
Among their veins, gone crooked over voyages,
Made by this ancient captain. Life has now
Contracted like the pupil of an eye
To a slit in space and time for images—

All he has seen of sage and arbutus:
Touched berries where the golden eagle crashes
From its chariot of air and dumb trap:
Islands fortunate as Atlantis was . . .
Yet while we thought him voyaging through life
He was really here, in truth, outside the doorpost,
In the shade of the eternal vine, his wife,
With the same tin plate of olives on his lap.

CAIRO

Cut from the joints of this immense
Darkness upon the face of Egypt lying,
We move in the possession of our acts
Alone, the dread apostles of our weakness.

For look. The mauve street is swallowed
And the bats have begun to stitch slowly.
At the stable-door the carpenter's three sons
Bend over a bucket of burning shavings,
Warming their inwardness and quite unearthly
As the candle-marking time begins.

Three little magi under vast Capella,
Beloved of all as shy as the astronomer,
She troubles heaven with her golden tears,
Tears flowing down upon us at this window,
The children rapt, the mauve street swallowed,
The harps of flame among the shadows
In Egypt now and far from Nazareth.

AT THE LONG BAR

Bowed like a foetus at the long bar sit,
You common artist whose uncommon ends
Deflower the secret contours of a mind
And all around you pitying find
Like severed veins your earthly friends . . .

(*The sickness of the oyster is the pearl*)

Dead bottles all around infect
Stale air the exploding corks bewitch—
O member of this outlawed sect,
Only the intolerable itch,
Skirt-fever, keeps the anthropoid erect.

Husband or wife or child condemn
This chain-gang which we all inherit:
Or those bleak ladders to despair
Miscalled high place and merit.
Dear, if these knotted words could wake
The dead boy and the buried girl. . . .

(*The sickness of the oyster is the pearl*)

BALLAD OF PSYCHOANALYSIS

Extracts from a Case-Book

Monday

She dreams she is chased by a black buck-nigger
But a fall in the coal-face blocks out the dream,
Something as long and lank as a lanyard,
Slow as a glacier, cold as cold cream—
Something inside her starts to scream . . .

Tuesday

Dreams she is chased by a man in a nightshirt,
Lawrence of Arabia dressed in a sheet:
Then locked by the crew of a Liberty Ship
With rows and rows and rows of refrigerated meat
While the voices keep repeating 'Eat'.

Wednesday

Dreams she is handcuffed to a dancing-partner
And dragged round a roller-skating rink.
She swallows the ring on her wedding-finger
Falls through the ice but doesn't seem to sink
Though her party clothes begin to shrink.

Thursday

Dreams she is queen of a mountain of cork,
Too hot to sit on, too cold to wear,
Naked, she pricks with a toasting-fork
A statue of Venus reclining there
With a notice saying: No charge for wear and tear.

Friday

She dreams she's a dog-team tugging poor Scott,
Sheer to the confines of the Pole:
Suddenly the Arctic becomes a-burning hot,
And when they arrive it's just an empty hole,
A geyser whistling in a mountain of coal.

Saturday

Dreams she's the queen of a city-culture
Lovely as Helen but doomed to spoil:
Under her thighs roll the capital rivers,
The Rhine and the Volga flowing like oil.
Hamlet offers her a buttoned foil.

Sunday

What has she got that we haven't got?
Isn't she happy and lovely too?
She dreams that her husband a bank-director
Locked in the Monkey-House at the Zoo—
Here's the clinical picture but what can we do?

THE OCTAGON ROOM

Veronese grey! Here in the Octagon Room
Our light ruffles and decodes
Greys of cigar-ash or river clay
Into the textual plumage of a mind—
Paulo, all his Muses held
Quietly in emulsion up against
A pane of cockney sky.

It is not only the authority
Of godly sensual forms which pity
And overwhelm us—this grey copied
From eyes I no more see,
Recording every shade of pain, yes,
All it takes to give smiles
The deathly candour of a dying art,
Or worth to words exchanged in darkness:
Is it only the dead who have such eyes?

No, really,
I think it is the feudal calm
Of sensuality enjoyed without aversion
Or regret . . . (incident of the ring
Lost in the grass: her laughter).

I should have been happy
In these rainy streets, a captive still
Like all these glittering hostages
We carried out of Italy, canvases
Riding the cracking winds in great London
Parks: happy or unhappy, who can tell you?

Only Veronese grey walks backwards
In the past across my mind
To where tugs still howl and mumble
On the father river,
And the grey feet passing, quiver
On pavements greyer than his greys . . .

Less wounding perhaps because the belongers
Loved here, died here, and took their art
Like love, with a pinch of salt, yes
Their pain clutched in the speechless
Deathless calm of Method. Gods!

BITTER LEMONS

In an island of bitter lemons
Where the moon's cool fevers burn
From the dark globes of the fruit,

And the dry grass underfoot
Tortures memory and revises
Habits half a lifetime dead

Better leave the rest unsaid,
Beauty, darkness, vehemence
Let the old sea-nurses keep

Their memorials of sleep
And the Greek sea's curly head
Keep its calms like tears unshed

Keep its calms like tears unshed.

EPISODE

I should set about memorising this little room,
The errors of taste which make it every other,
Like and unlike, this ugly rented bed
Now transfigured as a woman is transfigured
By love, disfigured, related and yet unrelated
To science, to the motiveless appeals of happiness.

I should set about memorising this room
It will be a long time empty and airless;
Thoughts will hang about it like mangy cats,
The mirror, vacant and idiotic as an actress
Reflect darkness, cavity of an old tooth,
A house shut up, a garden left untended.

This is probably the very moment to store it all,
Earlobes tasting of salt, a dying language
Of perfume, and the heart of someone
Hanging open on its hinges like a gate;
Rice-powder on a sleeve and two dead pillows
The telephone shook and shook but could not wake.

IN BRITAIN (X)

When they brought on the sleeping child
Bandaged on its glittering trolley
One could think no more of anecdotes:
Ugly Sappho lying under an acorn wishing,
Cyrano discountenanced by a nose like a wen,
My father's shadow telling me three times
Not to play with the scissors: None of this,
But of something inanimate about to be cut up:
A loaf with the oven scent on it exhaling
A breath of sacrifice, clouding the knife.

IN BRITAIN (XI)

Instead of this or that fictitious woman
Marry a cloud and carve it in a likeness.

IN RHODES (XII)

Incision of a comb in hair: lips stained
Blue as glass windows with the grapes
We picked and tasted by ourselves in Greece.
Such was the yesterday that made us
Appropriates of a place, club-members
Of an oleander-grove asleep in chairs.

INDEX OF FIRST LINES